COOL WOODS

A TRIP AROUND THE WORLD'S BOREAL FOREST

JANE DRAKE & ANN LOVE
ART BY ANDREW KISS

TUNDRA BOOKS

DEDICATION

To Irvin Batenchuk; Margaret Hudson; Johnny Johns; Ferrin, Randy and Vera Mitchell; Tony and Philomena Penashue, Josie Pone, and their families, people who shared with us their boreal home and captivated us with their stories.

J.D. and A.L.

To Lynn, the love of my life. Her support has made my career possible.   **A.K.**

ACKNOWLEDGEMENTS

The authors are grateful for the advice and guidance of Deirdre Baker, Henry Barnett, Ian Barnett, John Bidwell, Eric Butterworth, Jim Drake, Stewart Elgie, Jay Forsyth, Douglas Gibson, David Love, Bruce MacDonald, Guy Playfair, Steven Price, Ray Rabliauskas, Tracy Ruta, Stuart Slattery, Gary Stewart, and Cathy Wilkinson. Travel and research for this book was made possible by the generous support of The Canadian Boreal Initiative, Ducks Unlimited Canada, the Pew Charitable Trusts, the Innu Nation, and the Poplar River First Nation. Special thanks to our editor Kat Mototsune, publisher Kathy Lowinger, and the energetic, creative staff at Tundra Books.

Text copyright © 2003 by Jane Drake and Ann Love
Art copyright © 2003 by Andrew Kiss

Published in Canada by Tundra Books,
481 University Avenue, Toronto, Ontario M5G 2E9

Published in the United States by Tundra Books
of Northern New York, P.O. Box 1030, Plattsburgh,
New York 12901

Library of Congress Control Number: 2003102378

National Library of Canada Cataloguing in Publication

Drake, Jane
    Cool woods : a trip around the world's boreal forest / Jane Drake, Ann Love ; illustrated by Andrew Kiss.

Includes index.
ISBN 0-88776-608-0
    1. Taiga ecology--Juvenile literature. I. Love, Ann
II. Kiss, Andrew III. Title.

QH541.5.T3D73 2003   j577.3'7   C2003-901178-X

We acknowledge the financial support of the Government of Canada through the Book Publishing Industry Development Program (BPIDP) and that of the Government of Ontario through the Ontario Media Development Corporation's Ontario Book Initiative. We further acknowledge the support of the Canada Council for the Arts and the Ontario Arts Council for our publishing program.

Design: Cindy Reichle

Printed in Hong Kong, China

1 2 3 4 5 6   08 07 06 05 04 03

TABLE OF CONTENTS

FOREVER GREEN

Step into the woods. The wet ground – springy with moss – soaks your shoe. The soft-green needles of the spruce tree tickle the palm of your hand. Above, a chocolate shadow presses against the trunk. One wink reveals a boreal owl, daydreaming of voles and chickadees. Speckled summer sunlight catches a mound of dog-tongued lichen but misses a nearby wood frog. Shut your eyes and breathe deeply. A wild mix of skunk, damp mushrooms, and fragrant fir tingles your nose. Brush the mosquito from your ear and listen to the woodpecker's staccato beat.

These are the cool, northern woods that encircle the world. To return the hug, we are learning to care for them, the largest forest left on Earth.

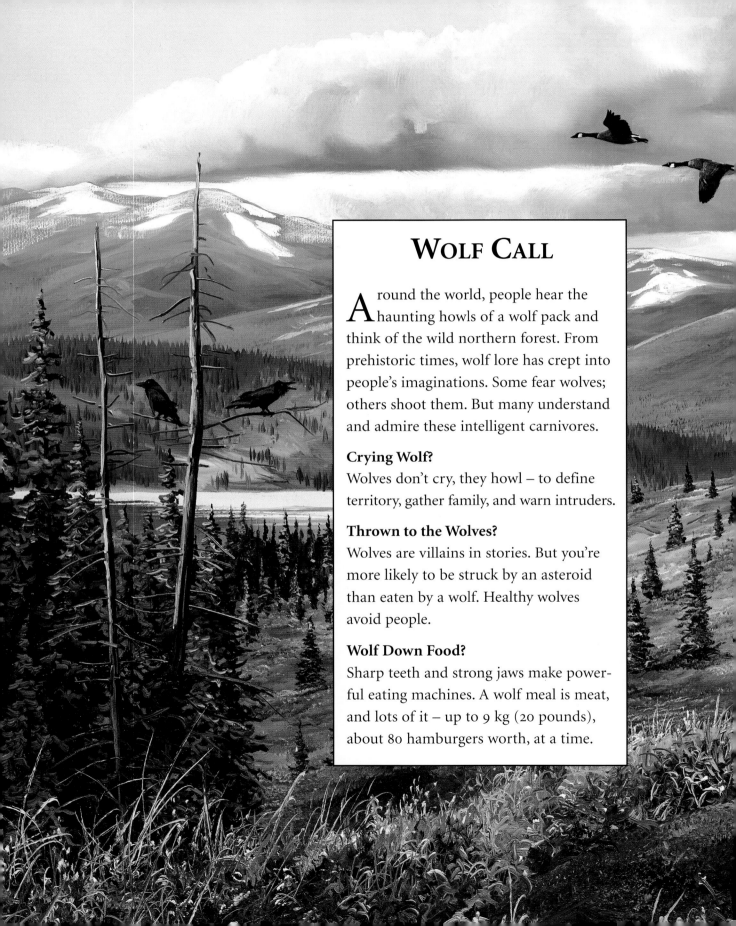

WOLF CALL

A round the world, people hear the haunting howls of a wolf pack and think of the wild northern forest. From prehistoric times, wolf lore has crept into people's imaginations. Some fear wolves; others shoot them. But many understand and admire these intelligent carnivores.

Crying Wolf?
Wolves don't cry, they howl – to define territory, gather family, and warn intruders.

Thrown to the Wolves?
Wolves are villains in stories. But you're more likely to be struck by an asteroid than eaten by a wolf. Healthy wolves avoid people.

Wolf Down Food?
Sharp teeth and strong jaws make power-ful eating machines. A wolf meal is meat, and lots of it – up to 9 kg (20 pounds), about 80 hamburgers worth, at a time.

WINTER IN THE WOODS

A still, bitter cold settles on the forest this January afternoon. The spruce trees stand rigid, resisting the occasional gust of wind. From its snow-covered branch, a red squirrel scolds a pine grosbeak as the bird snaps up the last frozen blueberry on a nearby bush. The temperature is well below zero and falling.

In the north woods, temperatures stay below freezing for more than half the year. And the ground is often snow-covered from October until May. With everything frozen for so long, winter is also dry. Yet resident birds and animals survive the meanest of winters, as do the trees that shelter them. Northern trees actually prefer long, dry winters. Coniferous spruce, fir, pine, and larch have adapted to the harsh climate in special ways:

Conical shape: Heavy snow slides off conifers rather than weighing down and breaking branches.

Needles: Trees lose less water through thin, waxy needles than through leaves.

Evergreen: Most conifers don't waste energy growing needles each year. And by staying dark green year round, the needles absorb some heat from the winter sun.

Shallow roots: The farther north you go, the longer the ground stays frozen in spring. In the farthest north, only the top layer thaws above permanently frozen ground, or permafrost. Northern trees have shallow roots that spread sideways to draw up water as soon as the ground surface melts.

Deciduous Survivors

Northern birch, alder, and young aspen are adapted to survive winter too. Their branches will bend in half before snapping under heavy snow.

FIRE! FIRE!

Springtime is fire time. The sun shines more than twelve hours a day. Dried by winter's wind, pine needles ignite quickly. Fire wipes the woods clean by devouring undergrowth and debris; healthy, sick, and weak trees; wildlife and insects. Native trees can take the heat – they're adapted to regrow after fire. Intense flames release seeds from hardy pinecones while ash enriches the soil and protects germinating seeds.

As the smoke clears, in move the wood-eating beetles. Beetle-eating wood-peckers quickly follow. Fireweed, berries, and grasses sprout from the ashes, and moose nibble their tender shoots. Aspen and birch send up new saplings from old root systems, and jack pine and spruce quickly reestablish. Ten years later, a diverse woodland community has taken over.

The woods cope with – in fact need – some fire. Small fires caused by lightning strikes are as natural as wind and snow. But human activities such as camping, road building, mining, and logging increase the number of fires. Some of these fires are monsters, roaring through the woods, destroying everything in their path as billions of trees go up in smoke. A warming world alters the forest's ability to regenerate after a fire, as higher temperatures and less rain hampers growth.

Satellite images lead water-bombers and skilled firefighters to forest-fire hot spots. But allowing small, remote fires to burn out on their own is one key to the future health of the forests.

THE GOOD FOREST

The north woods have many names. Some people call them *boreal forest* after Boreas, Greek god of the north wind. Others call them *taiga*, a Russian word for marshy woods, although many scientists save the word *taiga* for the wet, scrubby woods that border the arctic tundra. But to most northerners, the north woods are the *bush* – beautiful, wild, and full of trees.

From earliest times, people have gone into the bush for resources. They have hunted forest animals, collected firewood, gathered mushrooms and berries, and chosen strong, lean trunks for tent poles. Today, we still cut spruce to frame our homes. We use larch to make telephone poles and railroad ties; jack pine for sturdy posts, pilings, and timber. And fine white spruce gives special resonance to our musical instruments. But most of the northern trees we cut are mashed into pulp for making paper.

We also use the boreal forest by just letting it grow. And the boreal forest uses us. Like all living plants, trees grow by taking carbon dioxide from the air and releasing oxygen. Like all living animals, we do the reverse – our lungs take in oxygen and release carbon dioxide. The boreal forest is the biggest forest left in the world – bigger than the tropical rain forest. So, when you breathe, some of the air you inhale is likely fresh, sweet oxygen from the boreal forest. And some of what you exhale will eventually become part of a living boreal tree. That's why environmentalists call the boreal forest "the lungs of the Earth."

AROUND THE BOREAL WORLD

If you walked around the world through the boreal forest, you'd find few roads. As you bushwhacked through woods and wetlands, you'd notice many of the plants and animals were the same whether you were in North America, Siberia, or Europe. But you'd also spot important changes in the landscape and the kinds of trees and animals you were seeing. In places, you'd run into logging, mining, industry, and hydroelectric development. You'd also find people living off the land as their ancestors did. You might discover relics from early settlements – maybe even a ghost town. And in each community or homestead you'd meet people who tell their own exciting tales about the woods.

This book divides the forest into six sections or eco-zones — all boreal, but each with a life and story of its own.

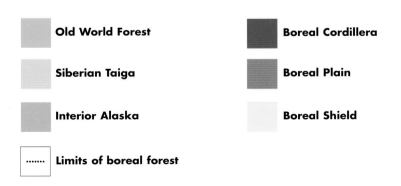

Old World Forest

Siberian Taiga

Interior Alaska

Limits of boreal forest

Boreal Cordillera

Boreal Plain

Boreal Shield

BOREAL SHIELD

Put on rubber boots and get ankle-deep in a damp world that's jumping with life. The boreal bog – where forest and water meet – is teeming with bugs, insect-eating plants, berry bushes, mammals, birds, frogs, minnows, sphagnum moss, black spruce, and more.

• Mosquito and other insect larvae hatch all summer long, feeding broods of ducks and other water birds.

• Sundew and pitcher plants snare insects – such as midges or dragonflies – in sticky traps, and digest the entire bug.

• Hardy western painted turtles live in the most southerly fringes of the Boreal Shield. They feed on aquatic insects and plants from early spring to late October, and then burrow into the mud for the winter.

• Standing stock-still in the shallows, a great blue heron waits patiently before stabbing a northern leopard frog with its yellow bill.

NATURE'S WOODWORKERS

The beaver, equipped with chainsaw teeth and amazing strength, changes the landscape faster than any other northern mammal, apart from people. When this hardworking rodent builds a home, it creates wetlands.

Beavers are selective loggers, choosing trees that happen to regrow quickly from underground roots. The branches, bark, and shoots are eaten or cached for winter. The trunks are dragged away to construct and repair lodges and dams. Beaver dams raise the water level and create marshland. Moose are attracted to beaver-made habitats, as are ducks, fish, and amphibians. All these creatures are inviting meals for predators such as wolves, bears, lynx, eagles, and wolverines.

Elegant adaptations help beavers survive the long winters of the boreal forest. The beaver family snuggles in the lodge, feeding from their stockpile. When supplies get low, they swim out to search for food. Fur and body fat insulate them, and layers of thick fur keep the icy water from touching their skin. Their ears and nostrils close tight, while extra eyelids protect their eyes. Their lips seal behind their front teeth as they carry branches back home.

Sculptors of the Woods

Pileated woodpeckers chisel cavities in trees for nesting and roosting. These crow-sized birds prefer old forests with a mix of live, standing dead, and fallen trees. Natural pest-killers, they catch carpenter ants and beetle larvae with their long, sticky, sharp-tipped tongues. Pileated woodpeckers help smaller woodpeckers by removing tree bark and exposing insects underneath. And, when they abandon their nests, flying squirrels, bufflehead ducks, or hooded mergansers move in.

A.Y. Jackson: Painter of the Northern Woods

Standing in snowshoes, his hands nearly too cold to draw, A.Y. Jackson holds his sketchpad. His charcoal pencil moves across the page, leaving broad, bold lines. When a beam of sunlight changes the color of the snow, he scribbles on his sketch, noting exact shades of gray, blue, green, yellow, and white. Back in his studio he'll transfer onto canvas the essence of Lake Superior's wooded shoreline in winter – cold, rugged, and very alive.

A.Y. joined the Group of Seven in 1921. This famous group of painters introduced Canada to the world, in particular the trees, rocks, and lakes of the boreal forest.

EN ROUTE

C'est l'aviron qui nous mène, qui nous mène,
C'est l'aviron qui nous mène en haut.

The chorus of this Quebecois folk song echoes off the rocky shore as ten voyageurs steer their birchbark canoe through the rapids. Soon it's dark, ending a long day's paddle. The voyageurs off-load the sacks of beaver pelts and haul the canoe ashore. The men tuck into stew warmed on the campfire, swallow a tot of rum, smoke a pipe, and roll into their blankets. Sheltered by overturned canoes, they sleep soundly until just before dawn. This was a good beginning to the seven-week trip from Grand Portage, Lake Superior, to the port of Montreal on the Saint Lawrence River. No one drowned, fell, or lost the cargo. And there were no bear scares on the 14-km (9-mile) portage.

A European fashion craze for hats made of beaver sent French fur traders deep into the northwest Boreal Shield and beyond. Native trappers exchanged beaver pelts and other furs for European goods such as rifles, axes, woolen clothing, pots, sewing needles, and thread. Voyageurs learned from Aboriginal people skills that helped them survive the long trips through the boreal wildlands:
• Dried pemmican (jerky made from moose or buffalo), wild rice, corn, peas, beans, maple sugar, and fresh berries were nutritious, fast food.
• When rocks, waterfalls, or shallow water slowed progress, portages (well-worn paths through the woods) connected the waterways.
• A canoe repair kit of spruce-root thread and pine gum for sealing leaks saved many an expedition.

- The best paddles were made of bois blanc – basswood.
- A smudge pot lit upwind helped keep insects away.
- Winter essentials included snowshoes, dogsleds, and toboggans.

BEST OF BOTH WORLDS

Across the Boreal Shield, many stands of forest have been clear-cut, flooded, or bulldozed for lumber, hydro, and mining development. But along the eastern shores of Lake Winnipeg, the people of the Poplar River First Nation actively protect their 800,000 hectares of unspoiled forest and traditional lands.

When the door to Margaret's store and restaurant opens, out rushes the rich aroma of moose stew and homemade pizza. The pizza is takeout for her brother's family; the stew for two visitors from the south. As her customers wipe their plates clean with bannock, she continues her story.

"I grew up here, in the bush," Margaret remembers. "We ate wild food and lived off the land. When a moose was shot, the meat was divided among neighbors and eaten fresh. We stocked up on staples at the Hudson's Bay store. Like now, there were only local roads, so we met few outsiders. But there was great excitement when the government dropped food and clothing packages from airplanes. My Grandmother made us underwear from the flour bags. When I went away to school at thirteen, I cried for four months. I hated being inside night and day."

Two grandchildren peek in the door and let Margaret know that Granddad's back from upriver. They bound off to meet his boat. "You know, we want the best of both worlds for those kids," she waves after them. "My children are raising their families in Winnipeg with French and ballet classes, but they come home for every holiday. Here in Poplar River, we teach the children respect for the old ways. So far, our Band has held firm against development of the forest. But at the same time, we now have a nursing station, warm homes, safe water, a school, and even a day care."

As Margaret clears the dishes, she observes, "It's a juggling act – balancing traditions with what pours in from the south by satellite TV and plane. But we're trying to get it right."

BOREAL PLAIN

The Boreal Plain is bounded by Lake Winnipeg in the southeast and the Mackenzie River delta in the northwest. Sitting between a rock and a hard place – the Boreal Shield and the mountains of the Boreal Cordillera – the rich soil of the Boreal Plain supports open forests of trembling aspen, white and black spruce, and balsam fir. Big mammals that have adapted to chilly summers and deep-freeze winters – caribou, grizzly, wolf, bison, and moose – thrive here year round, as do smaller creatures such as beaver, pine marten, and porcupine. Frozen for seven months of the year, the Mackenzie, North America's second-biggest river, keeps on ice much of Canada's freshwater reserve.

BOREAL BIRDS

Each spring and fall, tens of millions of birds clock billions of air miles flying through or to the Boreal Plain. What's the attraction? Many ideal combinations of food, water, and space exist here, appealing to a wide variety of species. From tiny, flitting warblers to loons and magnificent whooping cranes, the wetlands and open forest of the Boreal Plain offer migration rest stops, feeding grounds, and nesting sites.

These birds rely on boreal habitat to raise their broods. Without it, they'd face extinction.

Red-necked Grebe: Wetland Diver

Tailless, with legs and feet designed for swimming not walking, red-necked grebes are true water birds. Gathering in pairs or in colonies, they breed on shallow boreal lakes, rich with aquatic vegetation, insects, fish, and amphibians.

Palm Warbler: Spruce Bog Specialist

Palm warblers winter in the heat of southern Louisiana, but migrate north to nest in the brush of boreal spruce bogs. Wagging its tail with an up-down action, the male snaps up a marsh insect with its sharp, narrow bill. The female hides in the shrubbery, waiting for her eggs to hatch.

Whooping Crane: An Endangered Wader

Wood Buffalo National Park is the only breeding habitat for wild whooping cranes. Each spring, fewer than 200 birds migrate more than 4,000 km (2,400 miles) north from the Aransas Refuge in Texas, navigating around power lines, storms, and other hazards. Arriving as the ice melts, whoopers nest among the shelter of bulrushes. Here they raise one chick, feeding it insect larvae, clams, mice, and other marsh tidbits. By mid-September, the juvenile joins its parents on the flight south.

WOODLAND MEDICINE

Does your family have a remedy for hiccups, nosebleeds, or bug bites? Do you remember who you learned it from – your grandmother, an uncle? Ancestors of the Cree and other northern peoples found many ways to use forest plants for health and healing. Elders passed on valuable remedies to their children and grandchildren. Here are some traditional cures to minor ailments:

Child Care
• Diaper rash: Babies who wear clean, dried green peat moss called sphagnum on their bottoms are unlikely to get diaper rash.
• Teething: Parents can rub a cooked wintergreen leaf along sore gums to help relieve the pain of teething.

Bug Bites
• Mosquito bites: A cool wash made with yarrow leaves or a paste of trembling aspen leaves helps take away the itch of mosquito bites.
• Wasp stings: A paste made from birch leaves or wild rose petals helps relieve the pain of insect stings.

Wild Rose　　　　　*Aspen*

First Aid

• Minor cuts: Dry black spruce gum – cleaned, chewed, and soaked in warm water – can be used to protect small cuts from infection.

• Mild frostbite: A warm wet bandage made from the inner bark of a larch tree helps relieve frostbite.

• Hiccups: Chewing a wild mint called hemp nettle stops hiccups. And it also helps bad breath!

• Nosebleed: Pressing old man's beard lichen on the nostril helps stop bleeding.

Old Man's Beard Lichen

Serious Cures

Elders sometimes share their knowledge of powerful plants with scientists. Recently, this led to research into the active chemicals in birch bark, for example, as possible treatments for cancer, heart disease, and AIDS.

At Home in the Woods

Who wants a home where the buffalo roamed? Chilly and remote, the Boreal Plain has attracted a slow trickle of settlers over the last 200 years. And newcomers quickly learned, as the Aboriginal peoples have always known, that this is a no-nonsense place.

From north of Edmonton, Alberta, up to treeline, there's enough water, woods, and wilderness to fill several large European countries. Lakes and rivers provided summertime transportation, fish, and drinking water for the early homesteaders. Trees became homes, barns, fuel, and furniture, and the wild was a plentiful larder – for part of the year. Practical settlers who understood and adapted to the habitat did well; others perished or moved back south.

Survival Tactics

A family's first year in the wilderness was a race against time. Building homes required brute strength, sharp axes, and a faithful team of horses. Settlers used whipsaws to square and slice logs into rough planks. Women and children stuffed a combination of mud, grasses, and animal droppings between the beams to help keep wind and wildlife out. With luck and hard work, the family would survive their first winter in a small, smoky, dark cabin.

Before a garden was established, food supplies depended on the success of hunting, trapping, and fishing. Aboriginal people shared their cooking methods and recipes. Duck eggs were rolled in a tube of young poplar bark, which was plugged at both ends with mud and placed under hot coals for a few minutes. Another nutritious delicacy was warblefly eggs, plucked from the hides of freshly killed caribou and eaten raw.

PATCHWORK PLAIN

Picture the Boreal Plain as a big quilt, covering the earth as a unique ecosystem. Patches of forests, wetlands, open grassland, and lakes are stitched together by rivers. Many patches remain pristine, treasured by the people who live and work there. But some human activities punch holes in the fabric and unravel the stitching. Without strict regulation and care, the entire quilt could fall apart.

Edible Patches

The Plain's aspen woodland – once home to the northern long-eared bat, trumpeter swan, wood bison, and bay-breasted warbler – is overrun by grass. Pasture and grain fields are nibbling away at its southern boundary. So, with the northern edge defined by treeline, the Boreal Plain is squeezed. When forests are converted to farmland, temperatures rise, wildlife habitat is lost or limited, and chemical pesticides pollute soil and water.

Golden Patches

Buried beneath the Boreal Plain are patches of wealth – the world's largest uranium deposits, and sources of gold, silver, diamonds, oil, and gas. Many communities depend on extraction industries for their livelihood. But finding and retrieving these riches involves cutting even more trees each year than forestry companies harvest. Mining and drilling can affect waterways, air quality, wildlife habitat, and human health. And burning fossil fuels creates greenhouse gases that cause global warming.

Green Patches

Another threat to the boreal quilt is an endless demand for wood and paper. In the past, with the boreal forests seeming so vast and green, trees were clear-cut, threatening species such as grizzlies and moose. Now many forestry companies plan for the future by logging selectively and replanting for a continual, sustainable harvest.

PROTECT THE FOREST

Repair Patches

You can put a repair patch on the boreal forest by knowing what's what in paper and wood.

• Choose 100% post-consumer paper for computer printing and writing.

• Buy only books printed on Forest Friendly paper.

• Use a washable cloth instead of paper towels.

• Buy wood products certified as coming from sustainably managed forests.

• Recycle as much paper as possible.

BOREAL CORDILLERA

When you hike up a mountain trail, be prepared for some wild surprises. At any turn you could see an eagle soar or hear a marmot whistle. You might startle a flock of sheep or spot a perfect aspen leaf, shining like a golden coin.

Mountain forests have many habitats. A slope can face the sunny south or the shaded north. Depending on its drainage, the ground underfoot can be dry or wet. And the air always feels cooler the higher you climb. With each elevation change, look for new plant and animal sightings.

But stay alert and make a little noise. You don't want to surprise a bear!

LYNX AND HARE

A snowshoe hare flees across a clearing chased by a lynx twice its size. Will the hare escape or the lynx catch its meal?

Lynx don't always get their hare. In summer, the snowshoe hare's fur is gray-brown and blends into the forest floor. In winter, its outer coat turns white as snow. Well camouflaged, a hare sits still when danger approaches. But if it has to run, its large, bristled hind feet let it travel at nearly 60 km/h (more than 30 mph), even across deep snow.

Lynx are adapted to find and chase down hares. With large ear tufts, a lynx can pick up the softest sounds muffled by snow. And with keen eyes, it can detect any movement that might give away a hare's hiding spot. Lynx also have wide, snowshoe-like paws and long legs, just right for running through deep, powdery snow. Once a lynx flushes a hare, luck and skill decide if the lynx eats or goes hungry.

A snowshoe hare has about twelve young a year, plentiful prey for the lynx. Over several years, the number of hares actually increases until there are just too many. Then they run out of food, and many die of starvation. When the hare population crashes, lynx have less food and their population falls too. As the hares begin to recover, so do the lynx. This cycle of hare and lynx repeats itself about every ten years in the boreal forest.

SKOOKUM JIM, FROG WOMAN, AND WEALTH WOMAN

Skookum Jim was one of the lucky prospectors who found gold and started the Klondike gold rush of 1898. Jim earned the name Skookum, which means "strong," because he could carry heavy packs of bacon up the Chilkoot Pass. But his people, from the Tagish Nation, said it was his strengths as a family man and woodsman that shaped his fortune.

As a young man, Jim found a large frog trying to hop out of a dry ditch beside the Chilkoot Trail. Jim rescued the frog and carried it to a nearby creek. Soon after, the frog appeared to him as a beautiful woman and gave him a walking stick for saving her life. She promised the stick would lead Jim to gold.

Later, when Jim and his nephew were camped beside a mountain lake, they thought they heard a baby crying in the forest. They followed the sound – was it the wind? an owl? – but the cry kept moving ahead of them in the dark. Soon the nephew got scared and Jim walked him back to the tent.

The elders said that the crying baby belonged to Wealth Woman. Since Jim didn't catch up with her, they said he would never keep any wealth for long.

Two years later, Jim traveled to Dawson with his walking stick and struck gold, just as Frog Woman had promised. But, because he let Wealth Woman slip away, he spent all the gold in a few years. Jim was beloved until he died, and stories of his strength and luck are still fondly retold by his people.

BUSHED

After a hard winter digging for gold, would you climb a greasy pole, enter an ugly-face contest, or join a flapjack race? That's how miners whooped it up on May 24, 1899, in Surprise City, British Columbia.

Of the thousands who stampeded north hoping to strike it rich, few found gold and most left. But some settled, carving a life out of the bush. They built whole towns – post offices, saloons, hotels – with hand-hewn logs. They cut firewood to heat their cabins and to fuel their massive dredgers, sternwheelers, and sawmills. After backbreaking and often lonely work through buggy summers and cold winters, they felt bushed. Still, these miners knew how to have fun.

In the 1920s in Atlin, British Columbia, winter meant snowshoe picnics. Sometimes the lake froze with no snow – perfect for tacking a sheet onto a sleigh and sailing for miles. The lake stayed frozen into spring, making a smooth straightaway for bicycle riding! With summer came long hours of sunlight. Teams played baseball until midnight, and gardeners had fun growing record-breaking giant cabbages and pansies. Then autumn brought berry-picking picnics and fishing contests.

In the spirit of long-ago miners, today's Yukoners still beat the winter blues with Sourdough Rendezvous. Contestants compete to carry the heaviest packs of flour on their backs. Men shave clean on New Year's Eve and let judges decide whose beard has grown the bushiest by late February. And the lucky dog that pulls the sled piled with the most dog food wins a big dinner.

DOWNWIND, DOWNSTREAM

Do you own a bicycle, ski poles, ice skates, a skateboard, a TV, or a computer? Metals and minerals, used in making most modern equipment, often come from mines under the Boreal Cordillera. The mountains of British Columbia and Yukon are rich in gold, copper, silver, lead, zinc, nickel, tungsten, asbestos, cobalt, magnesium, and more.

No matter how careful miners are, they can't get ore from the wilderness to a factory without scarring the forest. They have to build roads to the mine site and construct a camp for the miners. Power-driven equipment is used to separate the ore from the rock and then concentrate it for shipment. This processing can pump toxic smoke into the air, and leaves piles of rock, called tailings, to slowly leach acid and dangerous chemicals into the groundwater. Then the ore has to be trucked out – more roads and more fumes. In all this activity, many trees are cut or bulldozed. Downwind and downstream, forests are exposed to air and water pollution. Meanwhile, boreal animals face new hunters and dangers.

PROTECT THE FOREST

Value What's Valuable

• You help the forest when you value your belongings made from mined products. REDUCE the number of disposable items you buy. REUSE any equipment in good condition. And REPAIR equipment when you can.

• Support local people, conservation groups, and governments when they work to identify and protect for all time threatened areas of the boreal forest.

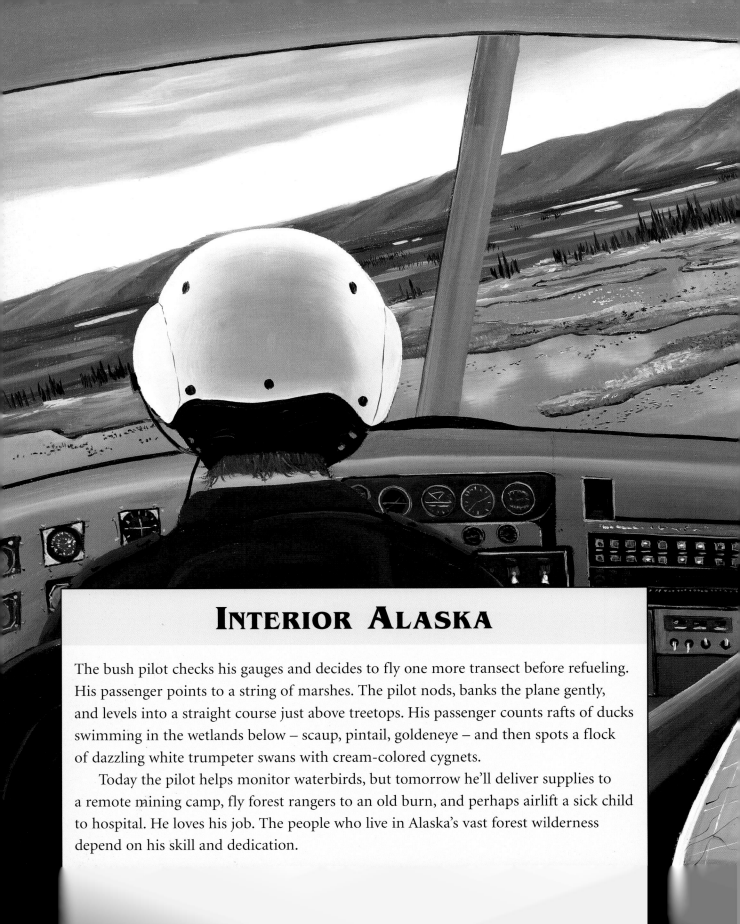

INTERIOR ALASKA

The bush pilot checks his gauges and decides to fly one more transect before refueling. His passenger points to a string of marshes. The pilot nods, banks the plane gently, and levels into a straight course just above treetops. His passenger counts rafts of ducks swimming in the wetlands below – scaup, pintail, goldeneye – and then spots a flock of dazzling white trumpeter swans with cream-colored cygnets.

Today the pilot helps monitor waterbirds, but tomorrow he'll deliver supplies to a remote mining camp, fly forest rangers to an old burn, and perhaps airlift a sick child to hospital. He loves his job. The people who live in Alaska's vast forest wilderness depend on his skill and dedication.

GRIZZLY WINTER

The Koyukon people of Alaska have deep respect for the creatures of the northern wild. They know that overwintering animals are powerful, alert, and intelligent – well equipped to survive the harsh subarctic cold.

The female grizzly, for instance, knows when to start gorging on sweet berries to bulk up for winter. She finds the driest, most sheltered site for her den. As November's drifting snow seals the entrance from the wind, she falls into a deep enough sleep to conserve her energy – but stays wakeful enough in late winter to give birth and care for her newborn cubs.

Meanwhile, tiny voles stay active all winter in tunnels they burrow in the loose, crystalline snow that forms under deep snow banks. They eat roots,

seeds, and grasses they have carefully stockpiled. The ermine is long, lean, and white in winter – the perfect shape and color to patrol the snow tunnels for voles to eat. When an ermine kills a vole, it cleverly moves into the vole's grass-lined nest.

Moose seek shelter from the winter wind in willow thickets. They have unusually long legs and walk by high-stepping through the deep snow. Moose browse on shrubs, twigs, and bark until spring, when they can eat the more nutritious water plants again.

As winter drags on, the creatures watch and wait for spring. People listen for the hawk owl deep in the forest. Koyukon elders say hawk owls tap on tree trunks in late winter and, if the sound lasts for a long time, winter will be long too. But if the tapping is short, spring will come quickly.

RAVENS IN THE NORTHERN SKY

Whether it's a cold, short December day or a long day in June, if you enter the north woods you can count on the company of a few tough ravens. Expert flyers, these bold birds call attention to their antics above the treetops with loud, croaking calls. No wonder Raven is featured in Alaskan stories about the sky.

He Rotates His Body: A Koyukon Story
The Big Dipper is a man who was forced to leave Earth after he dared to argue with Raven. His body slowly rotates around the North Star. You can tell the time and season by looking at him. For example, in mid-winter at dawn, his head points toward sunrise.

Raven Steals the Sun: An Athapaskan Story

Long ago there was only night, because a powerful man kept the Sun hidden. Raven decided to steal the Sun, but couldn't find a way inside the cabin where it was concealed. Noticing that a servant came out every day for fresh water, Raven turned himself into a spruce needle and dropped into the pail. Once indoors, the man's daughter swallowed the spruce needle in her cup of water. Down in her stomach, Raven changed from the spruce needle into a baby boy and was born as the young woman's child. Raven-boy was soon toddling around the cabin searching for the Sun. When he finally found it under a blanket, he turned himself back into Raven, snapped the Sun up with his beak, and flew out the smoke hole in the roof. Raven was so pleased with himself, he opened his mouth to croak triumphantly. The Sun fell to the ground and bounced up to shine in the sky.

BEFORE THE BOREAL FOREST

In 1979 near Fairbanks, Alaska, a gold miner unearthed the mummified legs of a prehistoric mammal. Miners often dig up fossilized woolly mammoth bones – but this creature was different. The legs had hooves, hair, and blue skin. A paleontologist carefully defrosted the body and dug it out of the frozen muck. He identified it as an extinct steppe bison, a huge, long-horned beast that lived in Alaska when the interior was cold, treeless grassland. A chemical reaction between the bison's skin and the mud had turned its skin blue. By performing an autopsy on the remains, scientists were able to put together the story of how it died.

In early winter 36,000 years ago, at least two prehistoric American lions attacked the steppe bison as it grazed in a valley. While one of the lions scratched and bit the bull's rear, another suffocated it with an airtight bite to the snout. For a few days, the lions ate the choicest meat from the back and rump. One lion lost part of a tooth trying to rip back the hide to expose more meat. When the body froze solid, the lions left. Ravens probably pecked out the eyeballs and, along with other scavengers, picked at the exposed backbone until snow covered the remains.

In spring, before it started to decompose, a mudslide buried the body. Underground, the bison's remains slowly mummified in the permafrost. Above ground, a spruce forest replaced the prehistoric grasslands. When Blue Babe was discovered, no lions or bison lived within thousands of miles. Instead, moose and wolf walked over its grave.

ROADS KILL

When top predators are doing well, their forest home must be in good health too. In most of Alaska, both predators and boreal forest are thriving.

The forest is healthy because few roads cut through it. When roads are built, people move in and secretive, wilderness-loving predators start moving out. First to go are wolverines with lynxes, martens, and wolves close behind. Roads attract construction projects and extensive logging that disturb migrating animals such as salmon. And when salmon are in trouble, so are the bears and bald eagles that feed on them.

By changing natural water movement and creating roadside ditches that direct water downhill, roads cause the forest to dry out. They also increase the chance of severe forest fires started by careless people, and Alaska doesn't need more fires than those that ignite naturally. Most of the boreal forest here grows on shallow soil containing wet, rotting vegetation called peat. In spring, when the peat and surface water are still frozen and the trees are dry, fires can ignite the peat and melt the permafrost just beneath. This changes the soils, the water levels, the sorts of plants that can grow, and the kinds of animals that will survive.

PROTECT THE FOREST

Be a Forest Advocate

You can help boreal forest everywhere by speaking up and questioning plans for unnecessary new roads. Where roads are needed, they must be constructed with care for the surrounding forest. Express your concerns to neighbors and politicians in a letter to the local paper, on a poster for a community bulletin board, or on a Web site.

SIBERIAN TAIGA

The Siberian Taiga is the biggest and – in winter – coldest of any forest left on Earth. The winter winds are so frigid that the larch tree sheds its needles just to survive. Siberians claim that, on cold days, words can freeze midair and hang there unheard until winter's end.

In spring, the forest roars with the cracking and flooding of ice breaking up on more than a million rivers. The larches sprout silky soft needles. Dwarf birch, lichen, and cranberry carpet the forest in shades of green. And the air hums with mosquitoes, midges, and flies. The summer-lush Siberian Taiga nurtures millions of birds – including Baikal duck, spruce grouse, and nutcracker – as well as mammals with young, such as wolf, sable, and chipmunk.

SIBERIAN TIGERS DON'T PURR

Separated from its herd, the young sika deer crashes through the birch forest in a desperate zigzag sprint. Four times its size and with deadly determination, the female Siberian tiger closes the gap. Springing effortlessly off the snowbank, she hits her mark, hauling the deer down. One bite to the neck and the chase is over. This time the tiger has won, and she drags her prey back to three hungry cubs. There won't be any leftovers.

The majestic Siberian tiger – largest of all cats – is perfectly at home in the taiga of far eastern Russia. Snowshoe-like feet, equipped with retractable claws, propel the tiger up to 80 km/h (50 mph) over snow. A white underbelly and throat, combined with fewer stripes and paler fur than other tigers, make excellent winter camouflage. An extra layer of fat and thickened fur insulate against the bitter cold. Unlike lions, tigers are solitary (except for females with cubs) and mark their territories with sprays of pungent urine and deep scratches on tree trunks.

Despite adaptations to life in the Siberian Taiga, the Siberian tiger has teetered on the brink of extinction for more than sixty years. Poachers risk jail for the enormous prices paid for tiger meat, bones, and fur on the black market. Habitat loss is an equal threat. Mining, fishing, logging, and fire have crisscrossed the tiger's traditional domain. Now confined to three reserves, their numbers have bounced back from a low of 24 in the 1940s to an estimated 430. But with clear-cuts ringing the reserves and local hunters competing for deer, elk, and wild boar, is it any wonder that Siberian tigers don't purr?

THE TRAPPER AND THE TIGER: A NIVKH STORY

A father and son journeyed into the Taiga to trap sable. They had set their snares and were relaxing inside their tent, when the father warned the boy to watch for tigers.

"I'm not afraid of tigers," the boy said.

They heard a thump outside, and the son threw open the tent flap. He looked right into the yellow eyes of a giant tiger.

"Who's not afraid of tigers?" it growled.

The father stammered, "I am," and ran away toward the village.

"Well, I'm not afraid of anything," the boy shrugged.

"Then, we'll wrestle," the tiger snarled, "and the winner will eat the loser."

The boy's mouth went dry. He tried to run out the door, but the tiger blocked his way. He tried jumping over the tiger, but it raised its head and blocked him again. So he bent down, and when the tiger crouched too, the boy leaped over its back and up a birch tree. The tiger followed so closely, the boy could feel its hot breath on his heels.

Suddenly the tiger slipped, and caught its neck between two thick branches. It dangled helplessly, swinging its paws. The boy saw his chance and climbed down.

But seeing the tiger limp and struggling to breathe, he thought, "What a beautiful animal! Why should it die?" He grabbed his hatchet and chopped at one of the branches until the beast fell to the ground.

The boy turned to run, but the tiger raised its head. "Stop. Please accept my gift."

The tiger walked the trapline with the boy and showed him how to set snares to always catch sables. The boy retraced his steps and collected a sable from each snare.

When the boy returned home, his father wept to see him alive and with his sled piled with sable pelts. The boy grew up to be a famous trapper – but he was always watchful of tigers.

REINDEER AFTERNOON

Siberia: 1500 A.D. An Evenk herder leads his sturdiest reindeer up a mountain trail searching for a tall stand of larch. He has bred and hand-raised these deer for riding and heavy packing. Even so, he is watchful. Earlier he passed sign of a bear and skirted it respectfully. He knows bears are dangerous in autumn, and one could be ahead.

The air is fresh and the trees shine in the pale sunlight. A small owl drifts across the trail – a good omen. With luck and hard work, the herder thinks, he will cut and trim enough poles to repair his winter tent, load them on the reindeer, and be home by dark.

The herder stops when one deer slows down, shakes its head, and flares its nostrils. He peers through the trees and sees a form. Too slight for bear. A wild reindeer has returned early from the north. If he kills it, they will have enough skin for his wife to make long-legged boots for his growing son. And meat to share with the elderly shaman. Stalking the animal and preparing the carcass will take many hours, but he'll sleep on the mountain and return to his family tomorrow.

The herder never imagines that, in 500 years, his descendents will live and work in factory towns. And that very few will hunt, herd, and breed reindeer in the traditional way.

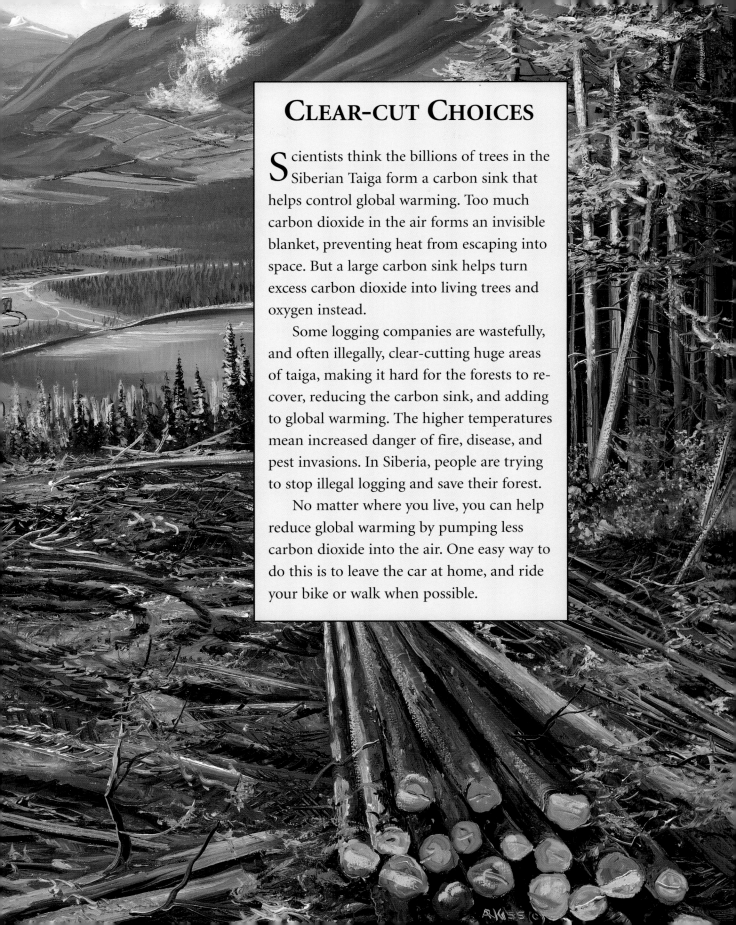

CLEAR-CUT CHOICES

S cientists think the billions of trees in the Siberian Taiga form a carbon sink that helps control global warming. Too much carbon dioxide in the air forms an invisible blanket, preventing heat from escaping into space. But a large carbon sink helps turn excess carbon dioxide into living trees and oxygen instead.

Some logging companies are wastefully, and often illegally, clear-cutting huge areas of taiga, making it hard for the forests to re-cover, reducing the carbon sink, and adding to global warming. The higher temperatures mean increased danger of fire, disease, and pest invasions. In Siberia, people are trying to stop illegal logging and save their forest.

No matter where you live, you can help reduce global warming by pumping less carbon dioxide into the air. One easy way to do this is to leave the car at home, and ride your bike or walk when possible.

OLD WORLD FOREST

Wearing a woolen dress trimmed with red braids and a reindeer-skin belt, the young Sami woman prepares to yoik – sing – as her grandfather taught her. She tilts up her chin, raises her arms, and slowly releases sound from her throat and mouth. There are no words, but her voice carries a story out into the night, across the snow toward the northern lights. Her tone rises and falls like dark mountains, rushes forward like the wind, sways with the trees, and scatters in every direction like midnight sunrays. She is remembering summer when reindeer nurse their calves, salmon fill the icy rivers, and cloud-berries ripen. Her family listens with their eyes closed, and they feel the warmth too.

SUPER WEASEL

The wolverine may be called glutton, devil beast, or skunk bear, but it's really a super weasel. No bigger than a midsized dog, a wolverine can haul down and kill reindeer, or drag a dead moose for hours. It's the terror of the northern woods.

Solitary scavengers, active night or day all year long, wolverines rarely seek shelter. Guided by their keen noses and warmed by extremely thick, frost-resistant fur, they scent and defend a large territory. Equipped with jaws like a steel trap, they can rip flesh, crush bone, and even saw through frozen meat. Their padded feet are ideal for running over snow, but slow them down on ground. In winter they kill anything that flounders in deep snow, and in summer they rely on berries, fish, and scraps left by wolves, bears, and people. When food is plentiful, wolverines slaughter excessively to cache and save for later. They routinely strip traplines of bait or catch. And they guard their food by puffing up their fur, baring their teeth, and growling fiercely.

Their reputation as ruthless predators is reinforced by their habit of wedging the heads of prey in the branches of trees. Trappers and reindeer herders have shot and poisoned wolverines close to extinction.

Nuthatches in the Old World Forest

Nuthatches live, eat, sing, and breed in boreal trees. Hopping right-side up or upside down, they hunt for insects, seeds, or nuts. After spearing their catch, they cram it in the grooves of bark, hammer it with their beaks, and eat the insides. And in winter, dozens of nuthatches huddle together in tree cavities, keeping each other warm.

SILVER MAID AND THE MILKY WAY: A SAMI STORY

I am known as the Sami Silver Maid and this is my story. As a young girl I watched the reindeer and taught myself to run as fast and sure as they do. Darting through the woods, dodging rocks and birch trees, I learned the local paths. The boys of my village chased me but could never catch me. They said whoever caught me would be my husband. I loved the challenge and taunted their efforts.

A fleet-footed youth from another village heard of me and decided to test his speed against mine. Close on my heels he pursued me around my well-worn pathways, but I kept one step ahead of him. Winded but still determined, he forced me off the trail and up a mountain. At the top there was nowhere to go, so I leaped into the air.

When I looked down, my suitor had collapsed in a heap at the summit, so I returned to Earth. Bending close, I heard his plea for water. There was none on the mountaintop, but I carried with me a reindeer skin full of milk. As I sprayed it onto his parched lips, the wind caught the milk and blew it into the air, forming a dazzling silver streak across the sky. Some splashed on my body, turning me to silver, hard and brilliant. My suitor revived and returned alone to our people. He told my tale, and now you know the Milky Way really is made of milk.

AN ENCHANTED FOREST

In the dead of a boreal winter there are few signs of life. Heavy with snow, the trees loom against the dim sky. No birds call or insects buzz. But northern Europeans know they're never alone. Whether they see them or not, they believe they're in the company of trolls, sea serpents, or Joulupukki.

Trolls

By night a big-nosed, wart-faced creature with wild hair and small fir trees growing out of his head; by day a lonely stone. Such is life for some make-believe trolls. Grumpy at best and dangerous at worst, a famous troll lives under a bridge in Norway. For 200 years he's plotted to eat the three Billy Goats Gruff, but the goats are still grazing on their mountain meadow.

Selma the Serpent

Lurking beneath the surface of Seljord Lake lives a mysterious creature with the head of a horse, crocodile, or elk and an eel's body that stretches from 3 to 30 m (10–100 ft) long. Does it knock fishermen from their boats and bite with deadly poison? When the surface boils with crisscrossed waves, is it diving to the bottom? Since 1750 there've been more than 100 recorded Selma sightings. But nobody has produced a shred of living proof. The trap's set and experts remain on standby for the first specimen. They may have a long wait.

Who is Joulupukki?

In Sweden, he's Jultomten; in Russia he's Ded Moroz. He's Pa Norsk in Norway and Joulupukki in Finland. But you might recognize him as Santa Claus. In the land of reindeer, Santa makes his home and workshop on Finland's Korvatunturi, a mountain in the shape of elf ears. From here, it's easy for Santa to hear who's naughty or nice. And there's plenty of lichen – every reindeers' favorite food.

SCOTLAND:

BRINGING BACK THE BOREAL

A small flock of Scottish crossbills descend on a stand of pine trees, calling "kip, kip, kip." Jostling one another for the best perch, they feed on ripe pinecones, snatching every seed with their hooked and crossed bills. Crossbills are as Scottish as kilts and bagpipes. When the Scottish Caledonian Forest all but disappeared, so did the crossbills. But with recent conservation efforts, the crossbill and other species dependent on this remnant of Old World Forest – capercaillies, crested titmice, pine martens, polecats, and red squirrels – have brighter futures.

Over the last 400 years, sheep and cattle farmers cleared most of the Caledonian Forest. Upper-class hunters stocked the countryside with red deer and pheasant – species that browse on seedlings. Fencing, home construction, and shipbuilding cost the forest more trees. Wood was burned in smelters for refining minerals, and forests were reduced by natural and human-caused fires. Finally, troops cleared woodland for Allied training grounds during the World Wars. Now less than 1 percent of its original area, there are only thirty-five patches of pine woodland left. Such massive habitat loss meant local extinction for wolves, bears, beavers, lynx, elk, aurochs, and reindeer.

Since the early 1990s, groups such as the Millennium Forest for Scotland have worked to bring back the boreal forest. Raising public awareness, establishing national reserves, fencing out deer, and cooperating with local people helps protect the remaining forest. And by replanting native species of trees, they may soon be able to reintroduce mammals that have been gone for decades. Long-term plans include connecting the forest fragments and establishing real wilderness. And with the gritty determination of the Scots, chances are good they'll succeed!

FOREST FOR THE FUTURE

Sarah lives near the shores of Lake Melville in Labrador. She goes to an English school, plays sports with friends, and watches satellite TV. And sometimes she spends weekends at her family camp in the bush.

Last visit, she woke up to the smell of bannock cooking on the woodstove. After breakfast, Sarah and her cousins collected fresh balsam boughs for the tent floor. They helped fill water jugs from a clear stream and carry firewood – all the while talking and joking in their Innu language. At the site of an old burn, they picked blueberries and ate until their tongues were as blue as their fingers.

They met an Innu forester who talked with their great-uncle about which hillsides were suitable for logging and which valleys should be protected. The forester gave his dog a sandwich and everyone laughed when a raven tried to steal it.

Back at camp, Sarah made a fort for her cousins to sit in and enjoy their partridge supper. As darkness fell, she snuggled into her sleeping bag for storytelling by candlelight. She learned that one of her ancestors, a shaman, could speak with the animal masters and find where to hunt caribou. She heard how her people tricked the guards at a military base so her aunts and uncles could erect a tent on the runway – in less than four minutes – to protest against fighter jets flying at low levels over tradi-tional Innu land. As the fire died down and an owl hooted nearby, Sarah thought she'd like to be a teacher some day – or maybe a police officer.

Despite threats from logging, pollution, recreation, and development, huge tracts of the boreal forest remain wild and healthy. Large numbers of remarkable animals and plants survive. People still live with the forest and respect it as their ancestors did. It is a place where old stories are told and new stories are born.

GLOSSARY

aboriginal peoples: original or first people in a region, such as Athapaskan, Cree, Evenk, Innu, Koyukon, Nivkh, Sami, Tagish
adaptations: modifications in the structure, form, or behavior of a plant or animal that help it better survive in its environment; e.g., the large paws of a lynx that let it travel on top of the snow.

bannock: a country bread made with baking powder instead of yeast and cooked on a campfire or woodstove
boreal forest: the circumpolar, subarctic forest that lies directly south of the arctic tundra and is made up mostly of coniferous trees. See *taiga*.

camouflage: the body covering a plant or animal uses to blend into its surroundings; e.g., the brown snowshoe hare's coat turns white in winter to blend with the snow.
carbon dioxide (CO$_2$): a colorless, odorless gas released into the air mostly through people and animals breathing and fossil fuels burning
carbon sink: a storage area of carbon, an element present in all living things. The boreal forest stores much of the world's carbon in trees, plants, peat, soils, and wetlands. It takes excess carbon dioxide out of the air and turns it into living trees and oxygen in the air.
clear-cut logging: where all the trees are cut down and harvested. Clear-cutting is often favored for economic reasons. Compare with *selective logging*.
climate: the normal or average long-term weather conditions of a region. In the boreal forest: short, warm summers and long, cold, snowy winters.
coniferous: cone-producing trees, including spruce, pine, and fir. In the boreal, all coniferous trees are evergreen except larch (or tamarack) trees, which drop their needles each fall.

deciduous: trees and shrubs that shed their leaves each fall, such as birch, aspen, poplar

ecosystem: a natural system formed by the interaction of all its living and non-living parts
elders: older, revered members of a community

fossil fuels: the remains of ancient plants and animals that are burned as fuel, such as oil, coal, and natural gas

global warming: a worldwide trend of increasing average temperatures
greenhouse gases: gases in the atmosphere, such as carbon dioxide, that block the escape of excess heat from Earth

habitat: a place that naturally supports the life and growth of a living plant or animal
hydroelectric: a kind of electricity made from the energy of moving or falling water. In the boreal forest, hydroelectric development means damming rivers, flooding forests, and cutting trees to make hydro lines.

lichens: small, simple plant-like organisms, part alga and part fungus, that commonly live on the boreal-forest floor, rocks, and trees

migration: seasonal movement of animals from one region to another. In the boreal, animals usually migrate to find food and shelter in winter.

permafrost: permanently frozen ground under the topsoil layer
poachers: people who illegally catch fish or wildlife
pulp: processed wood fiber, soft and wet, that is used in making paper, cardboard, and other wood products

selective logging: a kind of logging in which only certain trees are chosen for cutting in an area. Compare with *clear-cut logging*.
shaman: a spiritual leader who mediates between the human and spirit worlds

taiga: another term for boreal forest. Taiga is used for the whole boreal forest in Russia, and by scientists for the more northerly boreal areas in Canada. See *boreal forest*.
traditional: age-old, by custom. Traditional knowledge, beliefs, cures, stories, and ways are handed down from generation to generation.
treeline: where the forest ends and the treeless tundra begins

wetlands: areas that hold shallow water and/or wet soil at least part of the year, such as marshes and bogs. Some scientists say the boreal forest is so wet it is actually a giant wetland.
wilderness: a natural region inhabited by wild animals and undisturbed by people and development

INDEX